T0166509

STORIES
I AIN'T TOLD
NOBODY YET

STORIES
I AIN'T TOLD
NOBODY YET

SELECTIONS FROM THE
PEOPLE PIECES

— JO CARSON —

THEATRE COMMUNICATIONS GROUP — 1991

Stories I Ain't Told Nobody Yet is published by Theatre Communications Group, Inc., 520 Eighth Avenue, 24th Floor, New York, NY 10018-4156

This publication is made possible in part with public funds from the New York State Council on the Arts, a State Agency.

TCG Books are exclusively distributed to the book trade by Consortium Book Sales and Distribution.

Reprinted with the kind permission of Orchard Books, a division of Scholastic Books, Inc.

Library of Congress Cataloging-in-Publication Data
Carson, Jo, 1946–2011
Stories I ain't told nobody yet: selections from the people pieces / Jo Carson
ISBN 978-1-55936-027-2
1. Appalachian Region—Poetry. 2. Mountain life—Poetry.
I. Title.
[PS3553.A7674S76 1991]
811'.54-dc20
90-29030
CIP

Cover photograph copyright © 1984 by John Menapace.
Author photograph by Pat Arnow.
Cover design by The Sarabande Press

First TCG Edition, May 1991
Fourth Printing, November 2011

For Pierce

*With thanks to The Road Company,
the Center for Appalachian Studies and
Services of East Tennessee State University,
and Alternate ROOTS (Regional Organization
of Theaters, South).*

CONTENTS

PREFACE

WHAT FOLLOWS are monologues and dialogues collected from east Tennessee and the Appalachian region. They are not exclusive to the region. I made a woman angry once: she swore I got them from east Texas and just said east Tennessee. She was from east Texas.

The pieces all come from people. I never sat at my desk and made them up. I heard the heart of each of them somewhere. A grocery store line. A beauty shop. The emergency room. A neighbor across her clothesline to another neighbor. I am an eavesdropper and I practiced being invisible to get them. My aunt introduced me for a while saying, "Be careful what you say; she writes things down." I asked her not to say it. Blew my cover.

I did sit at my desk to reconstruct what I heard, so it was not that I hauled out notebooks on the spot and copied down people's words. The pieces are distillations. Some of these conversations took longer than others. Some took longer to write than others; one or two took years.

My intent has been to remain true to the speaker's thoughts and rhythms of speech and anything else that can be kept somehow in chosen words.

When there is a reference to another person, I have changed names. The layout on the page has to do with how the pieces should sound.

I have used these pieces in performance for several years. Doing them always seems to call up other stories. "You need to meet my cousin, he's got this dog. . . ." It's the thing I love the best about them. I hope it holds true for print.

STORIES
I AIN'T TOLD
NOBODY YET

PROLOGUE

1

Willis Comfort did not outlive
as many enemies as he hoped to.
I know because I was one of 'em.
I do not plan to do to his grave
what he swore he'd do to mine.

Grace or dying, one got Willis;
I hope it was the grace.
See, grace don't always come
on the wings of a dove
or as a thief in the night
or however it's supposed to.
Sometimes it comes like a two-by-four
to the side of the head
and folks don't live through it.

What can be said of Willis
can be said of everybody:
he made it through this world
the best way he knew how.

NEIGHBORS AND KIN

2

It's gettin' to where
you can't give a person nothin' anymore
and it's too damn bad.

Now, my neighbor
could look the devil in the eye
and say no thanks he didn't want to go to hell,
while at the same time
tryin' to slip Jesus Christ a couple of dollar bills
for the free gift of salvation.

He's a hard man
and he's about to drive me crazy.
Fifty cents he puts in my mailbox,
or a dollar or somethin',
and all I did was give his wife
a couple of tomatoes
and a mess of old string beans.

And they ain't rich.

Then, yesterday, I picked a half a bushel
of them little ol' zucchini squash
and I carried over five or six

and put them on his porch
with a note that said,
"These are a present."
Present was underlined.
And today,
there's a dollar in my mailbox.

The man don't understand
he's doin' a favor
when he takes and eats them damn zucchini,
and when he pays me for 'em,
when he pays me for 'em
it's me ends up beholden to him.

3

I spent the first years of my life
sittin' on what we called splinter benches
'cause we were too poor for store-bought furniture.
You scooted, you got splinters.
My mama used to cry
'cause she wanted a bed with a real mattress
for Grandma Lynn to die on.
Turned out Grandma Lynn didn't need it.
She died mid-sentence at the women's circle.
But the first money I ever earned
I got Mama a store-bought mattress.
Daddy bought her two straight-back chairs
so she and him could sit proper at the table.
It was her birthday.
I never seen anybody since
made so happy by a gift.

When Daddy finally found regular work
first thing they did was ride down to McEnniss's
and choose a houseful of fancy stuffed furniture.
Bought it on time, had it delivered, and paid for years.
The day it came, Mama and I stood out back
bustin' the old stuff with an ax.
Mama said if they couldn't pay for their bed
she'd rather sleep on the floor than have that one back.
We burnt furniture for kindling all that winter.
Mama'd say, "Here goes the table, Charlie!"
and she and Daddy'd laugh and raise their coffee cups
to toast their new prosperity.

Turns out we burnt what could have been
my fortune in antiques. My wife collects 'em.
She likes what she calls primitive;
it's the very stuff my mama didn't like,
and now I'm supposed to fix it so it don't ruin clothes
instead of bust it up.
I don't mind, might as well be this as something else,
but if I do get to heaven, if I do get to meet my mama
    again,
I don't know how in this world or that one
I'm gonna explain why I still got splinters in my seat.

4

Now, George is sick,
there ain't no question,
an' I've mentioned
for a year or so
about goin' to a doctor
an' he'd say
"Nooo, no, no."
But I'm gonna make 'im find one now.
It's really bad.
I mean,
George has got so sick
he don't even like
goin' to funerals anymore.

5

There was a story about my daddy's daddy
who bought a horse, a long-legged red mare
come from kin at Nashville who owed a favor,
and he worked and trained that horse to run.

Daddy tells of bets going up at the sight of that mare
and then money already changing hands
as Grandaddy come out of the saddle after a race
and give the mare to him to cool her off.
And tells about the two of 'em riding home,
a paper sack stuffed with winnings
when there wasn't room for it all in their pockets.

Daddy tells this story too:
the afternoon the red mare ran and won again
and Grandaddy climbed off her back and sold her
and they walked the six miles home to dinner
weeping, both of them, my daddy begging to know why.

The old man said horse-racing was the devil's work.
Said it had to be. Said they'd been having too much fun.

6

It was a Saturday and my mother was cooking.
She always cooked on Saturday
for us and for her bachelor brother
who came by on Sunday afternoon
and got his casseroles for the week.
None of them used tuna fish, mushrooms, peas . . .
there was a list of things he wouldn't eat.
We were not allowed to be so picky.

By Sunday they'd be frozen.
All he had to do was keep them frozen
and put them in the oven one at a time.
His were labeled, he knew what he was going to eat.
For herself, she looked into the frozen layers
and tried to remember.
I don't know why she did it.
He was perfectly capable of doing
anything else he set his mind to.
He could have learned to cook.

This Saturday
she was up to her elbows again in family and food.
I heard her in the kitchen. "No," she said.
After a moment: "I'm honored, but no thanks."
Another moment: "No, thank you, no, no, no."
I asked who she was talking to. She said,
"I'm practicing my speech for the circle,
they are planning to ask me to be president."

I thought she was very silly practicing
her public speaking with a series of emphatic no's
as she stacked casseroles in her freezer.
"No!" to the macaroni and cheese and tomatoes.
"No!" to the broccoli in concentrated celery soup.
"No. No. No."

It was twenty years before I understood
she was trying to learn how to say it.

7

It's not me
that's gonna stand up and say
Henry can't cook . . .

and you can look at Henry
and know he don't suffer
for the lack of food

. . . but I swear Henry don't cook
like nobody I ever knowed
had to eat his own.

You'd think he had a crow to pick,
put him some beans in a little pot
and cooks the fire out of 'em—
one speed, and it high,
and I swear to you
he don't call 'em done
until they start to smoke.

And he mushes up his scrambled eggs.
You ever heard of that before?

Henry's coffee gets boiled
till it grows little devils in it.
Now, I've been polite and drunk it
without sayin' anything,
but he don't keep no milk or sugar or nothin'
to cut the taste.

But that's not the worst.
The worst is that Henry thinks he makes cornbread.
It's what he calls it,
and to hear him talk,
you'd think he got the recipe from Chef Boy-ar-dee or
    somebody.
Now, anybody's got a skillet and some sense
can cook up cornbread,
and him carryin' on about his bein' so good . . .
Henry don't use bacon grease or buttermilk,
and that cornbread ain't got a prayer.
Anybody knows that.

Henry's dogs won't eat what's left over,
and dogs will eat good cornbread.

So I made up some right,
crunchy like it's supposed to be,
but not dry,
and I buttered it,
and I went over and invited Henry to come eat a piece,
just to know what good tastes like,
and you know, he wouldn't do it.
Said he just ate a piece of his own cornbread.
Said he wasn't hungry.
And I know better 'cause it was then
I saw what I saw in the bowls
where the dogs wouldn't eat it.
Henry is a liar!
But it ain't gonna be me
that says he can't cook.

8

How's Mama?

Who?

Mama.

Dead, Grandmother, gone more than forty years.

Well, tell me about Ruby.
She still a-runnin' that boardin' house?

I think the boarding house burnt down.

And Ruby died in the fire?

Died in Florida. Playing bridge.

And wanted to be buried with her bridge cards
and that boy of hers—what's his name?

Ben.

—he wouldn't do it,
said nobody made it into heaven yet with cards in their hand.
I said the Lord might like bridge once he learned to play it.

I heard you gave her a deck. I heard you walked
to a five and ten cent store during the funeral service
and bought a pack of Bicycle cards and put them
in the coffin.

What I should of give her was a push.
There wasn't no need of her goin' off to Florida.

Except to play bridge after Ben got religion.

When you reckon Paul'll get here?

Grandmother, Paul's gone too.

Gone huntin'. Him and Bennett and Jess.
We been waitin' a right smart time.

We're waiting for Jean.

Jean who?

Your daughter. She went into Kroger's
to get milk.

I told Paul to cook his squirrels where he shot 'em
'cause I didn't want to see 'em without their hide on.

You mean he died too, don't you.

And Bennett and Jess.

And Velma and Ellen and Lawrence and Thomas.
Who do I know that ain't already dead?

9

My brother Estes
and his cousin Ray
left here for California
the minute the two of them together
had enough money to buy a car.

They were leaving the god-forsaken mountains.

They were gonna make some money,
gonna find them California wives.
Well, they done right well,
both of them.
I gotta admit that.

But I got a phone call from Estes
just two days ago.
He's pushing into his fifties now,
and you know,
he wants to bring his California wife
and come back home.

All this time, he's called me
his hick sister,
I knew my chance was coming,
'cause the mountains speak the loudest
to a person in his middle years,
and no matter where he is
or what he's done,
he begins to think of them as home.

You know what I told Estes?
I told him to come on back and try it,
but not to get his hopes too high
'cause he don't talk right anymore.

10

A lady who lives there close to me
called me up the other day—
she'd had new carpet laid
and wanted me to come and
drink a cup of coffee and admire.

Now, I can do that for a person.
I hung wallpaper by myself one time
and come near to inviting a perfect stranger
in to see it. . . .

Well, I got to the door,
and she said, "Now you be careful
how you wipe your feet,"
and I was careful,
but the grass was still a little wet
from rain that morning,
and she asked did I mind too much
pulling off my shoes?

Well, I did that too,
and I stepped into the living room,
and that brand-new carpet was white. Bleach white.

And we drunk our cups of coffee in the kitchen.
The nicest thing I could think to say
was that it looked like snow nobody stepped on yet.

And I thought about how
there'll be no children
carryin' in chunks of chocolate cake
to watch TV,
no dog rollin' around to play
on the living room carpet,
no runnin' in that way
from sittin' on the front porch of an evening
to answer the phone,
nobody comin' in the front door
from workin' in the garden
or gettin' the mail
or carryin' through a handful
of cut flowers.

"It makes the room look really clean," I told her.

"That's what I like the best," she said,
" 'course I'll have to be so careful,
it being white and all."

1 1

You know the other day we went over at George's get some eggs?

    No, we went over George's get some beans.
    George ain't got eggs.

No, we got beans up at Lucille's.

    We took tomatoes to Lucille.

We took tomatoes to Wally.

    Where'd we get the beans?

Lucille's.

    I swear we took tomatoes.

Well, we didn't.

    Now, Wally's got a garden.
    Why we carryin' tomatoes up to him?

His ain't come in yet.

    Lester's has; Lester should'a give him some.

Lester's so tight you couldn't pry tomatoes out of him.

    He give George's boy a little puppy.

It was a stray and it turned around and bit him.

Who?

Lester.

Well, at least it wasn't George's little boy.

What'd we get at George's?

I guess we didn't go to George's.

Oh. Maybe that's why we ain't got no eggs.

1 2

Law, you know who's living
down in Jack's old house?
Lucy.
And Jack
and his family
moved down where
George used to live
before he moved out to the country.

Well, George broke his leg
and come back
and moved in with his cousins
right next door
to where I used to live
when you all had the house across the street.

Ritchies live there now,
where you lived.

Well, the people who lived
on the other side—
moved in after you left, I think—
they live in my old house now.
Has more yard.

Well anyway,
that house next door,
the one Lucy moved out of into Jack's old place . . .
Well, George ain't getting along too good
with his cousins right now,
and he's thinking about moving in.

1 3

You know Lou Beal?
Lives out close to you.

       Yeah, tall woman.

Now I never thought of her as tall.

       She's taller than me.

Maybe, but she's—you know—fat.

       Maybe she used to be and lost it all
       before I knew her.

Yeah. Well, her husband . . .

       I didn't know she was married.

I guess he's her ex. . . .

       Never mentions him.

She has children, don't she?

       Not out where I live.

Well, they must be with her husband.

2 4

Well, anyway, her husband said . . .
I reckon they must be gettin' back together. . . .

What'd he say?

They're fixin' to move to Indiana.

14

She come to see your mother
said she knew your mother
was laying in the bed six weeks
but she hadn't felt up to
walking through the Morelock's yard.

Said her liver don't work
her bladder leaks
her hair is falling out
and her heart's half dead

so I asked her
                    don't it stink?

15

About them whiskey boys:

Jim Beam will lie flat out
and George Dickle'll tell you
you can dance.
Don't believe either of them.
You can trust Ezra Brooks to put you under.
Evan Williams will remind you in the mornin'
what you done that night.
And Jack Daniels,
Lord, that devil Jack Daniels . . .
make you wish for things
you never even thought about before.

OBSERVATIONS

16

Mountain people
can't read,
can't write,
don't wear shoes,
don't have teeth,
don't use soap,
and don't talk plain.
They beat their kids,
beat their friends,
beat their neighbors,
and beat their dogs.
They live on cow peas,
fatback and twenty acres
straight up and down.
They don't have money.
They do have fleas,
overalls,
tobacco patches,
shacks,
shotguns,
foodstamps,
liquor stills,
and at least six junk cars in the front yard.
Right?

Well, let me tell you:
I am from here,
I'm not like that
and I am damned tired of being told I am.

17

There are some things I want to know about,
I want to know what happened to the trees.
There used to be big trees,
big enough you could hollow you a room inside
and live inside a living tree
without a whit of difference to the tree.
They were everywhere.
Them trees was big enough
you could of made two floors
and carved a staircase up
and slept inside the middle of a tree
if you had a mind to work like that.
It wouldn't hurt the tree.

Them trees are gone,
but trees don't die for just two hundred years.
Old trees move slow.
Each spring is one more morning
and goes a thousand years
before a tree begins to look at getting old.
Them trees are gone.

These here, these little ones
they're good to climb
'cause you can get your arms and legs around
and shinney up the children of old trees.
But this place is not a forest.
It's bramble breaks and laurel hells.
It's good to have for hunting in.

It used to be the lower limbs and branches
of the trees stood above the ground
at eight or ten men's height,
and in the forest was the only place
where you could see along the ground.

18

You can always tell a tourist town.
Everybody wears blue jeans,
men and women,
fancy expensive ones—
with stitching on the sides—
or made to look like
clothes that used to work the land
but don't in tourist towns.

Free spirits in blue jeans
drive small cars
with bicycle racks
or ski racks
or surfboard racks
or luggage racks
or fancy pick-up trucks
and park them in rows.
(The line of license tags reads like
a recitation of the fifty states.)
They seek to buy the Promised Land
on the slopes,
on the surf,
in the sun,
in the shops,
in the bars,
or in some decorated tin cup
offered by the locals
(also in blue jeans)
who used to think

the Promised Land might really come
when, at last,
the cars from fifty states
filled up the parking lots.

19

One day
I'm gonna write a letter
to those folks in Washington.
You know what I'm gonna say?
I'm gonna say,
"We don't need no more roads."

We got more roads now
than we fill up potholes on . . .
and ever'where you look,
there's some new one goin' in.

What I'm gonna tell those folks up there is this:
There's roads enough right now
that people wants to live on big ones can,
and people wants to live on little ones can do that too.
More big ones is gonna get more people,
more little ones is gonna get more people,
and we don't need no more people.

Most of all,
we don't need no more new roads.

20

It's changing here.
I know it.
Everywhere you look
somebody's putting in
a new road,
a new house,
a new business,
a new something-or-another,
and I know we're growing,
we need some of that . . .
but we're changing
the beauty out of things.

It's not like
you can't tear down
a mountain.
Anymore, you can
and people do.
So what's one mountain,
more or less?
Level off the tops,
we might have something to farm.

I never thought much about progress
until now,
and I certainly never thought of myself
as against it,
but it's turning out I am against it.
And it's not because progress is bad.

It's because progress—
the way we're doing it—
is so ugly.
A mountain is beautiful.

I'm young
I know that,
and probably rash,
but I swear
I hope I die
before the only thing that's left
that takes your breath away
around here
is the smell.

21

The first time I sat in a restaurant
where blacks were not served
Martin Luther King was still alive.
I knew I would not be served;
I knew it would be me who served
time in jail. I had taken a shower
and eaten my lunch in preparation.
When I came to consciousness
I had vomited my lunch,
I had been beaten and handcuffed
to the bars of a cell in the city jail.
I stayed in that position for a week.
I had a wound on my head
that needed medical attention.
It was not the last time I sat
where blacks were not served.
I did it until I was sentenced
to the federal pen or the U.S. Army,
my choice, and I served in Vietnam.

M.L.K. was murdered twenty years ago.
My daughter is almost the age I was
and we were sitting in a restaurant
where blacks are not served.
There was no sign that said white only,
there was a waitress who behaved
as though she could not see us.
"We're color blind in America,"
my daughter said and we walked out.

Black people already know this story
and who else do I think might listen—
the woman who refused to see us?
the couple who came in after we did
who were served when we were not?
This story is not newsworthy, nobody
needed stitches, but this is the same story
as the one that cracked my head open.
The only thing that changed is the law.

2 2

I want to know when you get to be from a place,
five years, ten, twenty?
What about when you find a place you love?

"But honey, where are you from?"

It is a discriminatory question,
and it turns up everywhere
including job applications.

I am from three states
and six different cities.

I am from Interstate 40.

I am from the neighborhoods
where people moved every other year.

I am from the work my father did.

I am from the things I hang on my wall
and the bed I get out of in the morning.

I am from that suspicious minority
that doesn't have roots like trees.

I have lived here eight years,
and the mountain I see when I wake up is imprinted—
like a duck, I know my mother when I see her.

Can you earn being from a place?
I work, I vote, I help my neighbors, I pay taxes.
Can I pledge allegiance?

People would do better to ask
where are you from of Eastman
or Nuclear Fuels Services
or the waste management company
that left the toxic dump in Bumpass Cove.

And if the identity is so precious
they should ask it of Kroger
and K-Mart and Long John Silver's.
But it never goes that far.

It just goes to the property boundary
when my neighbor steps back a step and says,
"Oh. You're not from here are you?"

RELATIONSHIPS

2 3

Either of them young'uns married?

      Nope.

Well, they're old enough ain't they?

      How old you figure's old enough, old man?

Well, reckon you're right. A girl ought
to wait a while before she goes
gettin' herself married. . . .
Takin' on a man and a family,
it ain't easy,
and she don't want to tie herself down
too soon, now does she. . . ?

      If you're askin' me a girl ain't never old enough
      to marry.

24

I had a beautiful wife—
    compared to what he's got.

The woman had her faults—
    if you know what I mean—
but they weren't nothing to the faults
his woman's got.

The truth is this:
I couldn't live with my wife,
but I wouldn't have tried
to live with his.

25

You know,
all along I've been back here
playing second fiddle.
Like I thought I was supposed to.
And twenty years goes by.

And I turn around.
And find the first chair sittin' empty.
Has been all along.
Got cobwebs in it
old enough to petrify.

First chair's out
on permanent coffee break
except he don't know how
to brew his own.

He's plannin' on findin'
somebody else to do it.

I'm gonna buy me
a new set of strings for this old fiddle
and sit down in the first chair for a while.

I expect we find out
who can carry a tune in a bucket
and who can't.

26

Forty years we courted . . .

> Thirty-nine.
> Now, my mother didn't like Jack . . .

. . . and Amy wouldn't marry . . .

> . . . well, I couldn't without her consent
> and her so close to dyin'.

It took her thirty-nine years
and she died of old age.

> But we always thought,
> and you too . . .

. . . that she was on the edge.
She always said . . .

> She thought Jack would leave me.
> Well, twenty years proved her wrong.

Yeah, and the second twenty proved her stubborn.

> She worried, Jack.

Ah, I know.
Like to of killed me.
But we endured.
We did that and we've done more.
We've loved each other for forty years.

Well, three days ago, my mother died
and we're announcin' our intent . . .

. . . to marry.
So long a waitin' makes the moment awful sweet, Amy.

That it does.

27

I threw my mother-in-law out.
She made me mad
trying to tell me things
ain't none of her business.
I told my wife—
we been married four weeks—
I told my wife
to tell her
I'd had enough
and I didn't wanna see that woman again.

And you know what she did,
my mother-in-law?
She said
she's gonna tell her old man
to come and take the car back.
And I told my wife
to just let her.
Damn car don't start anyhow.
Have to jump it off
ever' time you want to go somewhere,
and it with a new battery.
I had to put a alternator in it
just this morning,
and it still don't start.
And I got forty dollars in new used tires on it.

Well, she did call him
and I called him and asked him
if he's gonna try to come and get it,
and he said he wouldn't,
but I told my wife to just let him.
He ain't gettin'
the battery
or the tires
or the alternator
and he's gonna have a hell of a time
draggin' that car
out of the parkin' lot.

28

My daughter got divorced
and she and her little boy
has moved back in with me.
For the time being.

And everything she goes to do,
she's got a book.

Gonna cook something,
she looks up in the book
to see what she wants
and then when we ain't got it,
she's got to run out to the grocery store.

"I'll just be gone a minute, Mama, you keep Chip."

Now, we got hamburger meat
and we got beans
and all the rest of the stuff
you put up from a garden,
and there's been many a soul
to make it through this world
without ever tastin' veal scallopini.
I could have done without it.

And she made herself a dress.
First she read the book of sewing machine directions,
then she's got this other book
that tells her how to make things.

Took two days for something
that might of taken me two hours.
I said that.

"But I did it right," she says.

Then Chip put a towel down the flush commode,
and she read *The Reader's Digest Fix-it Book*
while the damn thing flooded up the bathroom.

"I didn't know how," she said.

You see, that book
don't tell about straightening out a coat hanger
and fishing something out.

"Not everything's got a book written about it," I told her.

"I know that, Mama, there wasn't a book written about my
        marriage.
I might not be here if there had a' been."

Now what am I supposed to say to that?

29

I cannot remember all the times he hit me.
I might could count black eyes,
how many times I said I ran into doors
or fell down or stepped into the path
of any flying object except his fist.
Once I got a black eye playing softball.
The rest were him. Seven, eight.
I can name what of me he broke:
my nose, my arm, and four ribs
in the course of six years' marriage.
The ribs were after I said divorce
and in spite of a peace bond.
I spent the night in the hospital.
He did not even spend a night in jail.
The sheriff I helped elect does not
apply the law to family business.
He always swore he never meant to do it.
I do believe he never planned.
It was always just the day,
the way I looked at him afraid.
Maybe the first time he did not mean to do it,
maybe the broken ribs were for good luck.

I want to post this in ladies' rooms,
write it on the tags of women's underwear,
write it on coupons to go in Tampax packages,
because my ex-husband will want to marry again
and there is no tattoo where he can't see it
to tell the next woman who might fall in love with him.
After six months, maybe a year,
he will start with a slap you can brush off.

Leave when he slaps you.
When he begins to call you cunt and whore
and threatens to kill you if you try to go
it will almost be like teasing but it is not.
Keep two sets of car keys for yourself.
Take your children with you when you go.
If he is throwing things, he is drinking.
If he is drunk enough he cannot catch you.
A punch in the breast hurts worse than a punch in the jaw.
A hit with an object does more damage than a hit with a fist
unless he is so drunk he picks up a broom instead of a poker.
If you pick up the poker, he will try to get it.
If he gets it, he will hit you with it.
He probably will not kill you because you will pass out,
and then, he is all the sudden sorry and he stops.
When he says he will not hit you again
as he drives you to the hospital,
both of you in tears and you in pain,
you have stayed much too long already.
Tell the people at the hospital the truth
no matter how much you think you love him.
Do not say you fell down stairs
no matter how much he swears he loves you.
He does love you, he loves you hurt and he will hit you
    again.

WORK

30

This is the only junkyard in this county.
Ain't it beautiful?

I spend ever' Friday and Saturday night
goin' to auctions to get this.
I buy careful:
money don't grow on trees around here,
and I got just about everything
a body needs.

I specialize in hubcaps
but I got good stuff,
wire and clothes and locks and coffee cups
and tools and pots and furniture.
You name it, I got it or I'll get it,
and I'll sell it to you at the salvage price.
See, it don't matter to nothin'
but the angle of a person's nose
whether somethin's been used before or not.

I run a kind of service too.
You tell me what you want
and if it ain't here already,
I'll keep an eye out. No extra charge.

55

31

Don't talk to me about no options; I'm poor.
. . . them talking about choosin' one "lifestyle" or
   another . . .

I get to choose
between pinto beans or navy beans at the grocery store,
between rats or roaches where I live,
between the used coats at the Salvation Army.

I get to choose
whether me and my kids are going to be hungry
or I'm gonna get food stamps.

I get to choose
the work I'm goin' to do,
whose john I'm gonna wash which day of the week.

That's the choosin' I get to do
'cause I ain't learned in schools
and now I got four young'uns.

But I am educated.
I know when somebody's talkin' trash
ain't worth feedin' to hogs.

3 2

I've worked this place
over and over again,
year in, year out
tryin' to grow a livin' on it.
And I do. Used to be a decent livin'.
Not anymore but I'm still a-livin' on it.
This patch of ground
or this fellow one is tired out.

I could make more money
takin' up tithes at the poorhouse.

My son, he got himself a job
at that plant that makes the rubber gloves.
If he'd ever quit for long enough
we might could get this place goin' again.

I asked him would he think on that.
He said there's easier ways
of breakin' your back than scratchin' in dirt.

3 3

Oh my good Lord, I am not a young man anymore.
I have spent my life at work
I felt might help to keep things whole.
It tears my soul when I see
the earth spoiled for money,
for some small increment of time,
or because it doesn't fit a plan . . .
some tom-fool set of words on paper
conceived behind desks in offices with no windows.
Behind a desk, there are no fish in water.
There are numbers, and percentages die
with certain concentrations of heavy metals
or changes in temperature, not fish.
There are no pictures of floating dead on office walls
and references to the food chain might as well mean
another billion whoppers passed through the golden arches.

I write and no one reads
or worse, someone does read
and the scientific language numbs the brain.
I say some fish by the Latin name
"contains five times federally accepted standards
of mercury contamination in its muscle tissue."
Who gives a damn? I cannot say
eating that fish contributes to your death.

I have not helped to keep things whole.
I have done my work, I have loved the earth,
but I didn't start shouting soon enough
or loud enough and now all shouts are muffled
by the volumes of paper the likes of me produce,
or else there are no ears.

Who gives a damn? Me. I do.
I used to think I knew some answers or could find them. . . .
I had some ways, some knowledge,
and a saving grace, the scientific method.

It may be the ultimate in cruelty jokes—remember them?—
to write what could be without exaggeration
the beginning to the end of life
in some small creek, not to mention some small planet,
and to watch some bureaucrat tear the research up
and say, "Get me some other figures;
that set doesn't fit the plan."

3 4

I used to work down
the dye section,
hey, hey. . . .
They paid me good too.
A hundred and fifty's a awful lot
to carry home with you
every week
thirty years ago.
But I quit.
I'd come back home from Detroit
to take that job
and I quit.
They told me I was crazy
'cause I couldn't make
that much money anywhere else
and they were right about that,
but let me tell you,
it wasn't crazy,
it was scared.

I used to wake up
middle of the night
and whatever side I'd been sleepin' on
I couldn't feel it,
couldn't move,
and I'd think it's just me
and wait for a while
and the feelin'd come back.
But one afternoon
down at the plant,
this boy—

he worked on line,
now I didn't work on line—
but this boy froze up.
His arms locked up
in front of him
and it's a week
before he got the feelin' back.

And I got to thinkin'
maybe it wasn't just me
feelin' so funny of an evening
and I quit.

Now, I'm telling you the truth,
I'm seventy-four years old
and it's been thirty year
since I worked down there,
but you know somethin' . . .
of them that stayed
and a lot of 'em was younger than me
but of them that stayed
there ain't one alive today
to tell about it.

Right after I left
I thought,
Lord, you're crazy, Lee,
leaving a job
pays so good.
And I went down
to Florida

bummin' around awhile
'cause I couldn't find work.
But I'm alive,
I am alive,
and I feel awful funny sometimes
about them that ain't.

35

I've been at that job
four year
and if I stay twenty more,
I can retire okay.
And it ain't too bad for line work.
It's heavy though,
lifting sheet pieces
and hookin' 'em up.
I already hurt my back some,
and the edges are too sharp.
I'll lose a finger or two
before it's over,
I know I will.
I just hope
I don't lose
no arms or legs or nothing'd
disable me.

A finger's nothing,
my dad lost parts of three of his
on a job,
but a hand or a arm . . .
I hope that don't happen to me.
I'm kinda attached to them, you know.

Just have to step careful, I reckon.

36

Come times sometimes,
I look back.
I reckon everybody does.
I realized
I never really made
any big decisions.
Not basic ones,
not for myself.
I never asked myself
whether or not
I really wanted
to stay with this.
I just assumed I did.
I might have thought of that
some thirty years ago.
Instead, I made the hundred million
little decisions,
the time consumers,
the ones that lead to glasses
and to headaches:
Can I pay an extra hand?
What do I plant where this year?
Who do I try to sell it to?

All those.

Well, I sit here
and I dream
what would have happened
if I'd turned
some little one

of those decisions around,
where I might be
and what I might be doing.
But I'm not.

And then I think
I grew up here,
I have lived here,
worked here,
and I have made
all my decisions
about here and for here,
and in those many moments
I have kept my family together
and in health,
I have lived in harmony and good union
with my friends and neighbors
and I have kept
a piece of earth
in working order.
I am proud of that.

37

Twenty-one years,
long enough to grow one of two children
to the age of her majority,
I scheduled the machines, the space
and the people on the floor for Kingsport Press,
and when they terminated me
they sent a man who had been there
two and a half months
to thank me for my years of service.
All I could think to say was
I resent this.
Now, I can think of plenty more.

I was terminated because I earned too much.
They will re-name my job—
they cannot do without it—
and pay some new man less to do it.
It is a complicated responsibility
and for a while, he will lose them more money
than I cost. But not for long enough.
The valuable employee awards I got—
the last one was last year—
have turned into a bad joke.

Now, I get the opportunity to clean out my office.

I get severance pay if I sign a form that says I will not sue.

I get what I contributed to my retirement, no more.

I get to write a resume.

I have never felt so faceless or so used.

For the next person who pats me on the back
to say a rotten deal, a crying shame,
or some other easy whitewash
that does not say what happened
I have some new words: try injustice,
say abuse out loud.
And to those who will not look at me
because somehow fired and failed
are too close together,
bend over this barrel, friend,
your turn is likely to be next.
And for all who've never thought to ask it,
a question I never thought to ask till now:
who decided money is more valuable than people,
and why did all the rest of us agree to work that way?

38

I worked there as a secretary.
I wasn't there when they lost uranium—
that was when they hit the news—
but I had friends who felt like
it was a sloppy operation even then.
There were days when you went outside
and something in the air would make
the nylon hose melt off your legs.
You'd step out and seconds later
you'd be wearing holes with webs between 'em.
They kept hose for us free.
There were days I lost two pair.
Somehow the two pair days put me over a line
I hadn't really thought about at one pair.
I took up driving forty miles each way
to another job. I don't know yet
what it was that ate the hose but I guess
there's good news. Friends who work there
say it doesn't happen often anymore.

39

I have a direct mail business which means
I stuff a lot of envelopes.

And the mornings fifteen thousand pieces
looks like several thousand more than I can do

I start naming
the people I don't work for by doing this.

Rod Wilson and I stuff a flyer in an envelope
Jeffery Honeycutt and I stuff another one.

Ed Boswell, Joe Gregory, Tom Cook, Warren Jones.
It don't just help me do the work.

Naming those boys gets it done.

WE SAY OF OURSELVES

4 0

I want to tell,
a person can't help if they're not so pretty as the next.

All of us are given different things
and the gift God give to some of us
ain't always lookin'
like we just come out of a beauty shop.

Now, I don't mind.
I got what I want.

But I always told my mother
that teasing me about always lookin' so awful
was goin' to make me mean. . . .
And it did.

41

The day I married, my mother
had one piece of wedding advice:
"Don't make good potato salad,"
she told me, "it's too hard to make
and you'll have to take something
every time you get invited somewhere.
Just cook up beans; people eat them too."

My mother was good at potato salad
and part of the memories of my childhood
have to do with endless batches made
for family get-togethers, church picnics,
Civitan suppers, Democratic party fund raisers,
whatever event called for potato salad.
I'd peel the hard-boiled eggs.
My mother would pack
her big red plastic picnic bowl
high with yellow potato salad
(she used mustard),
and it would sit proud on endless tables
        and come home empty.

What my mother might and could have said is:
Choose carefully what you get good at
'cause you'll spend the rest of your life doing it.
But I didn't hear that.
I was young and anxious to please
and I knew her potato salad secrets.

And the thousand other duties
given to daughters by mothers,
and sometimes I envy those women
who get by with pots of beans.

4 2

I was born three months before I's due,
then I turned around
and got pneumonia
and then when I was nine,
I had leukemia.
I did.
I fell off'en a horse
and broke my neck
and lived.
And I went to war.
And since then,
I've wrecked two cars
and walked away,
clipped the wings off an airplane
landin' it,
and run out of a house afire.
I wiped out on a motorcycle
doin' about a hundred.

I been married full four times,
middle two liked to 'a killed me.

The fourth one's doin' alright so far,
except she keeps a-tellin' me
to be careful,
that I'm gettin' old.

43

Ain't no hell on earth
like small town lonely
where every person
knows where you've been
and what's happened to you,
and every one of them
made their decision
once or twice
about whether you was right
or wrong
in what's gone past.
And everybody but you
knows how their mind's made up.

The most you ever get
from any of them
is the time of day.
It's just that
some folks smile when you ask them,
and some don't.

44

Broke
is not sissy-footing around
saying, "I can't, I'm broke,"
holding a twenty-dollar bill in your pocket,
or
hollering about being
down to the wire
with a dollar or two in the checking
and a whole wad's not been touched
in the savings.

That's poor-mouthing.

Broke
is out of all liquid assets
including the ones in the pop-tops.
Broke
is cruising the house
looking for something to sell.

Broke
is when I hock
my daddy's rifle.
You can ask me
where's the gun,
and if it's down at Bud's,
you know the times are bad.

Really broke:
Hock money's run out and no more credit at the bar.
I sell whatever I'm driving.

Broke and in trouble with the law:
I put the red truck up
and borrow money against the title.

Never got down no worse than that.

45

Used to be just fine with me
to go out huntin'
till last year my husband came home
with a little eight-point buck.
He was so pleased.
"Big enough to mount," he said.
And he took the head along to the taxidermist.

Well, I cooked that deer,
roasts and stews,
and we had company in
'cause Lowell was the only one around
that got a kill that season,
and there was all the huntin' talk around the table,
who got what,
who lost what,
and who's gonna get what all next year . . .
you know them kind of stories . . .
and me just laughin' right along,
laughin' and cookin' and eatin' right up to the afternoon
Lowell brought the head back home.

He hung it over my piano,
and I swear it is the saddest thing I ever saw,
so dead and out of place.

I told Lowell then
that I couldn't stop him killin' one again
but not to bring it home
'cause I won't cook it
and I won't eat it
and I don't want no part
of the death of another deer.

I look at that head
every time I sit down at my piano.
And I'll tell you—
it's just about taken up my happy songs.

46

Every time I get a little headache
my daughter tells me
I shouldn't take these BC powders. . . .
She says, "Mama, you know
how that does your stomach."
And of course I know how that does my stomach.
It gets my little ulcer all in a fit.

And then my daughter says,
"Mama, you shouldn't drink that milk,
you know it gives you headaches. . . ."
And of course I know that too
but I have to do somethin'
for the little ulcer
'cause the BC's are so hard on it
and the milk does get down in there
and coats my stomach.

But then I am allergic to the milk.
Gives me headaches.

And then I do have to go
and take another BC powder.

And then my daughter starts in about
"It's a vicious circle,"
and "You're chasing your own tail,"
that kind of thing. . . .

What she don't understand
is that a person does
what they have to do.

And all that hecklin'
don't help high blood pressure
the least little bit.

47

Aw, lemme tell you,
this bachelor stuff,
it's great.
Out from under Mama.

I'm just about moved in
my new place.
Would'a been sooner
except there was some water standin' in it
and all my junk would'a got wet.

It don't matter to me if they fade some, where do I load 'em
    in?

Now, Mama's good,
she'd fix your food,
but she always has to know where you been.
"Where you been, it's twelve-thirty, where you been?"
Mama has to know.

Where do I put the money in this thing?

"You been drinkin', you drinkin' licker?"
She wants to know.
Of course, I been drinkin',
don't everybody?
A few beers after work to start,
and you know how it goes. . . .

This machine still don't start. Where's the button? Oh.

No more "Go comb your hair."
No more "Go change your clothes."
No more askin' where I been.
No more "Bring down your dirty laundry" either,
I do my own.

Hey, where's the soap? Don't they put the soap in these
    machines?

Well, it don't matter
'cause I'm gonna throw away
all them old sewed-up things anyhow.
I'm working now.
I can buy 'em new.
Ass-patched blue jeans ain't gonna be my style no more.

48

I ain't had no night,
ain't had no day,
ain't had no two weeks, either.

Hell, I ain't had no month when you come to it.

The dog choked,
the car wrecked,
the old man died
(course, we'd been expectin' that),
and now,
I got a broke toe
come from where
I dropped a skillet on my foot.

Ain't had no month to speak of,
that's the truth.

If the next one don't get better,
ain't likely gonna be no me
to speak about it.

Amen.

49

I lived off old 42,
up Cook's Holler,
through the gap
and down Limestone Creek a ways . . .
where it forks, you take the red side,
cross the bridge
and run a mile or two
along the foot of that little hill
where they didn't build
the road across 'cause of who owned the property.
It used to be a yellow house.

Now, would that have been the way
you'd 'a got to Christiansburg
if you had to go?

50

    Honey, you drive
two weeks to yesterday out 58
turn up the creek at Richmond's Bend,
turn down two miles in at the fork,
turn left at the blue and black Buick,
and come to the end of the road.
12 miles from where you're sitting.
    Step on it
and we'll wait dinner for you.

51

My brother died sitting
at the dinner table.
He had to be surprised.
I know he hadn't planned
for mortality right then.

He wasn't much for plans.
He liked making deals.
Jewels, pocket watches,
a knife if it was old,
and wives, three in all.
He'd dig in his pocket
for change to buy a coke
and bring out diamonds
every time and show 'em,
tell how he just got back
from "a buyin' trip."
Mexico, he'd say, Peru.
I never did believe him.
He went to Las Vegas
getting married and divorced.

Neither of us ever had
much luck with women.

I'd say he got the diamonds
at the same flea markets
he got the wives, the watches
and a pocketknife he swore
belonged to Jesse James.

His latest woman called me
when he died, said somebody
had to come to sign stuff,
said he had not left a will
and asked when the time came
to divide the property,
could I find it in my heart
to speak for her?
Said they'd planned to marry.
Said his ex-wives had
already hired lawyers.

I told her to hold her horses,
I wasn't adjusted to him being dead.

When I got in at the airport
nobody was there to get me,
nobody was at the house,
the girlfriend's stuff was gone
and I couldn't find no diamonds.
I had to call up funeral homes
to find out where his body was.
The only folks who came to the buryin'
were all the ex-wives's lawyers.

5 2

I watched the first sunrise
I remember seeing last week.
I am thirty-five.

I'm up at sunrise, I have
a job that ruins my wrists
and two children.
By sunrise, I am already busy.

Once, I sat awake for
a month of sunrises
that began with a call
from the youngest: Mama . . .
The child got so sick
he would not open his eyes.
His room faced west,
I watched—I counted—sunsets.

He is thirteen now
and mows for spending money.

So, Saturday, my husband and I
left the house before dawn.
It was my birthday, my choice,
my present, we went fishing.

I love fishing.

The pain was in my wrists
but casting a fishing line
is not the same as
dis-assembling chickens —
that's their word for it —
on a factory line. My job.

There we sat, me shivering,
in the dark with the crickets
and a rim of bright pink
lit the mountains so quickly
I didn't notice it coming.
It looked like an accident.
What's that? I asked.
This sounds so foolish now.
That light. "The dawn,"
my husband said and laughed.
I wept, I couldn't stop myself,
I don't ever remember seeing
a sunrise before.

"Happens every morning,
where on earth you been?" he asked.

Cutting up chickens.
Raising children.

5 3

When I die, I want to lay here
next to Mama and whisper
how sorry I am you took her.

      Next to Mama?
      Why should you be next to her?

There's lots of space.
You can be next to daddy.
Or over next to Hubert.
That's the prettiest view.

      I'm the one took care of Mama.

You took her to the hospital.

      I saw how sick she was.

She didn't want to go to the hospital.

      Her life was made up
      of things she do not want to do

Now I'm not saying the hospital
was what killed her but

      and sometimes mine is too.

I did know any wish could be her last
and she did not wish to go to the hospital.

She asked me to move her,
said you were a'smothering her,
said she couldn't get no rest
but what you woke her up
to make sure she wasn't dead.

She was delirious!

Either way, she needed more help than she was
getting.

I want her to know I tried to keep her
and I am sorry . . .

Oh, hush.
Mama don't want to hear that
any more than I do.

I want to lay next to her so I can say it.

You better plan to wait awhile
cause I'll make sure you have to shout
from over next to Hubert
if you die first.

54

I am asking you to come back home
before you lose the chance of seein' me alive.
You already missed your daddy.
You missed your uncle Howard.
You missed Luciel.
I kept them and I buried them.
You showed up for the funerals.
Funerals are the easy part.

You even missed that dog you left.
I dug him a hole and put him in it.
It was a Sunday morning, but dead animals
don't wait no better than dead people.

My mama used to say she could feel herself
runnin' short of the breath of life. So can I.
And I am blessed tired of buryin' things I love.
Somebody else can do that job to me.
You'll be back here then; you come for funerals.

I'd rather you come back now and got my stories.
I've got whole lives of stories that belong to you.
I could fill you up with stories,
stories I ain't told nobody yet,
stories with your name, your blood in them.
Ain't nobody gonna hear them if you don't
and you ain't gonna hear them unless you get back home.

When I am dead, it will not matter
how hard you press your ear to the ground.

ACKNOWLEDGMENTS

"Broke . . ." *Southern Exposure, July/August 1982; Now and Then,* Fall 1984.

"The day I married . . ." *An Ear to the Ground,* Athens, Ga.: University of Georgia Press, 1989.

"Every time I get a little headache . . ." *Appalachian Journal,* Winter 1983; *Now and Then,* Fall 1984.

"I ain't had no night . . ." *Southern Exposure,* July/August 1982.

"I am asking you to come back home . . ." *An Ear to the Ground,* Athens, Ga.: University of Georgia Press, 1989, and *1986/87 Anthology of Magazine Verse and Yearbook of American Poetry,* Beverly Hills: Monitor Book Company, Inc., 1988; revised version of "I am warning you to come back home . . . ." *Southern Exposure,* March-June 1985, special issue entitled *Southern Elders.*

"I cannot remember all the times . . ." *An Ear to the Ground,* Athens, Ga.: University of Georgia Press, 1989.

"I threw my mother-in-law out . . ." *Appalachian Journal,* Winter 1983.

"I used to work down the dye section . . ." *Southern Exposure,* July/August 1982.

"I want to know when you get to be from a place . . ." *Now and Then,* Summer 1986.

"I was born three months before I's due . . ." *Appalachian Journal,* Winter 1983; *Now and Then,* Fall 1984.

"It's gettin' to where you can't give a person nothing' . . ." *Southern Exposure,* July/August 1982; *Now and Then,* Fall 1984.

"Law, you know who's living . . ." *Southern Exposure*, July/August 1982; *Now and Then*, Fall 1984.

"Mountain people . . ." *Southern Exposure*, July/August 1982.

"My brother Estes . . ." *Appalachian Journal*, Winter 1983.

"One day I'm gonna write a letter . . ." *Southern Exposure*, July/August 1982; *Appalachian Journal*, Winter 1983.